THE X FACTOR
SELLING SYSTEM

THE X FACTOR SELLING SYSTEM

The Sales Expert's Guide to Selling
2nd Edition

To inspire greatness

THOMAS F. LA VECCHIA, MBA

With
Deanna Dunsmuir

&

Celebrity Plastic Surgeon
Dr. Ramtin R. Kassir

X Factor Selling Systems
Summit

The X Factor Selling System
The Sales Expert's Guide to Selling

X Factor Selling Systems books may be ordered through booksellers or by contacting:

www.thesalesexpertusa.com
Or
X Factor Selling Systems
55 Union Place
Suite 130
Summit, NJ 07901
908-377-6906

ISBN: 978-0-615-82668-4

Printed in the United States of America

Layout & Design by Anthony Piscitelli

Thank you to the people who have shown me the way and for all of those people who encouraged me to write this book. This book is dedicated to my beautiful wife Rosalia, and my two children Felicia and Giuseppe. Also, without the guidance of my mother Felicia La Vecchia none of this would be possible.

FOREWORD

"When the student is ready, the teacher will appear"

By Celebrity Plastic Surgeon
Ramtin R. Kassir, MD

The first day of my internship in surgery, my senior resident told me, "Do it now, write it down, and make no excuses". The medical process was tailored to the individual physician doing everything, from drawing blood to chasing down CT scan results. Years later in private practice as my business grew, I didn't know much about leadership other than fear and intimidation. I was frustrated to say the least, and realized that there were skill sets that I didn't have, like management, process, and metrics. I needed help, and that's when I met Tom La Vecchia.

It was interesting accepting the help because I thought I was smart (having set up the business on my own). His X Factor System (designed to help with the big picture from topics like leadership to time management and budgeting) gave me the inspiration to learn the skill sets I needed to get to the next level. X Factor was focused on establishing the systems to make our operations seamless so I had more time to be a physician. It was tantamount to getting practical business education.

So I learned to balance working on the business with working in the business. Tom helped me focus on my vision, and created core systems to see that vision to the end.

These systems encompassed hiring and recruiting, quality control and metrics, branding and marketing, and financial reporting and budgets.

I had to become more formal, more professional, and more technical as my business grew; had I not done so I would have been buried with more work and lost the most important things – the reason we go to work in the first place – to live. So if you're reading this book, it's probably time. The teacher has appeared.

INTRODUCTION

Just starting out in your sales career? My colleagues know me as The Sales Expert, and in this book, I share what I've learned throughout my career as a sales representative and as a sales manager. After reading The X Factor Selling System, you will have gained the equivalent of my twenty years of experience in the business.

This book gives you the basics of the X Factor Selling System. For those of you who want more in-depth training, I have created an E-learning platform and also offer seminars and one-on-one coaching.

My process is simple: After using four purchasing categories to identify why someone buys, you will then find the X Factor. The X Factor is the root cause of why someone purchases or says 'yes'. From there, closing the deal is the easiest part of the sale.

This book is targeted toward beginning levels and even serves as a refresher to expert sales associates.

What is your boss looking for from you? How will you meet and exceed your sales numbers? How will you know if this career is right for you? All of those questions will be answered in The X Factor Selling System, putting you ahead of the curve.

Table of Contents

CHAPTER ONE: "ENOUGH!"

*"The single biggest problem in communication is
the illusion that it has taken place"*

George Bernard Shaw

TEN YEARS AGO I was entering the South Bronx to make
my first pharmaceutical sales pitch. Except for attending a
Yankees game, I'd never been to the South Bronx. I remember
thinking that the city would either kick my ass or become the
platform to my success. I was 26 years old, with nine years of
experience working from a home office of a large pharmaceutical
company in suburban New Jersey. Essentially, I was isolated
from the outside world, and this was the time to make my mark.

Stuck in traffic, the oil from the El Train leaking onto my
windshield, I repeatedly went over what I was trained to say. I
was nervous, but having an innate ability to connect to people
and a solid knowledge of my product, I felt the sky was the limit.

Walking up to the door I wasn't sure if I was about to walk into
a low-rent Jersey DMV or a medical clinic. As I entered the
treatment center I saw about 100 patients awaiting the best care
they could find in the South Bronx. A wave of cockiness overcame

me as I took security in my education and sales training; I had just finished up my undergraduate degree and was currently seeking my MBA. Feeling confident, I strutted to the front desk, my business card in hand, and asked to see the physician in charge.

The 20-something-year-old girl behind the desk snickered.

"We typically don't see reps so you must be new," she said, snapping her gum.

"I'm not a rep, I'm Tom La Vecchia, from a large pharmaceutical sales company," I said, still holding onto my self-confident buoyancy.

She should have turned me away, yet she let me back- probably out of pure amusement.

As I walked back, down a small corridor, there were nearly 100 more patients waiting to be seen by merely two physicians. The care providers were stretched thin to say the least.

I approached the first physician I saw.

"My name is Tom La Vecchia and I am here to partner with you in order to best treat your allergy patients," I asserted, while handing him my card.

He took the card and began to walk, so I continued at his pace along side of him and explained my product in the fashion in which I was trained. Together we walked about 100 feet from where I introduced myself, when he slammed down my card with all of his might and screamed on the top of his lungs, "ENOUGH!"

Now I am thinking, *what the hell did I do?* I assumed based on my education, training and overall demeanor that I could make this sale.

But it was really pretty simple, I was unimportant to this customer. My product at that office was as useless as I was faceless to that doctor. How could I have handled that differently? Was it about being a bad rep or was it the way I was trained? How could I have made myself more valuable in the eyes of this potential customer that had 'ENOUGH!'?

Looking back, I can understand where I went wrong. If I had been using, what I later developed in my sales career, the X Factor Selling System, I could have made my sale that day. And I will explain later on how I eventually made a sale to that particular care center with my method years down the road.

What steps do you take after a situation of defeat?

_____

_____

_____

_____

How do you motivate others to act?

_____

_____

_____

xxxx

In this book you will learn the four-step process of the X Factor Selling System. You will learn how to price a product, how to see through a client's or a competitor's aura of legitimacy, insight into the mind of your sales manager, and finally if this career is right for you.

By using the X Factor Selling System, which I strongly feel is an improvement over current sales systems, you or your sales team will become exponentially more successful. Representatives I have coached-many of which I am content to say are lifelong friends-have made an added 30 percent on their incentive compensation within three months as a result of employing this model. After using this model as a sales manager with four different sales teams, whose regions spanned across various geographies and consisted of diverse products, all showed exponential growth in sales given a six-twelve month time period.

CHAPTER TWO: WHY DO PEOPLE BUY? THE FOUR P'S AND THE X FACTOR

"The subconscious is ceaselessly murmuring, and it is by listening to these murmurs that one hears the truth."

Gaston Bachelard

IN ORDER TO FIGURE out why a person buys, you must first find out their motivating factor (their X Factor). The X Factor is the root cause of why someone purchases or says 'yes'. In order to find someone's X Factor you will have to identify which purchasing category your client or target falls under. They will fall under one of the four P's: People centric, Product centric, Process centric, or Price centric. This is your target's cause of purchase. From there, you will dig deeper to find out why they fall under that category-this is their X Factor.

The Four P Centrists

People: Someone who falls under this category is relationship oriented and may say things like: "I bought this car because I liked the guy" or, "I only buy my fruit from Stephanie the grocer." It's about trust between two people and there is an emotional bond between the two parties.

Possible X Factors:

- Feeling the need to connect to a person to connect to a product.
- Having a lack of friendships or personal relationships.
- Wants to feel specifically important.

Process: People in this category will often take the path of least resistance. For example, physicians are creatures of habit as they are notorious for doing what is "easiest". On the retail side, convenience stores may charge more for making your life "easier" or a person may go to a to Jiffy Lube out of convenience (it is quicker, on their daily route, and they do not need to get out of their car while it's being serviced, etc.).

Possible X Factors:

- Feels they are too busy and/or do not have enough time.
- Falls easily into habit forming routines.
- Feels they need to preserve their energy/time for elsewhere.

Product: Whether it's a premium priced product or the least expensive, this person has product or brand loyalty. There are various reasons for this– whether it's a positive experience, a fashion statement, or having great utility. This is different from process centric because buyers will stick to a particular brand and its line/brand extensions – e.g. Gucci shoes, sunglasses and bags – aka product/brand loyalty. To further differentiate: a process centric person needs a coffee every day at 3 p.m., while a product centric person needs a Starbucks coffee.

Possible X Factors:

- Feels a certain line or brand is superior; focused on status.

- Likes what a line or product puts into their brand.
- Feels a certain brand is 'the best'.

Price: Someone who falls under this category is simply looking to get the lowest price. For example someone skimming the shampoo isle and choosing the cheapest shampoo, despite name brand or who is selling the product. Another example is someone looking to get the cheapest gas prices; the attendant does not need to be nice to you, or sell the best quality gas, they simply need to have the lowest price per gallon for you to purchase their gasoline.

Possible X Factors:

- Feels getting the lowest cost means good business.
- Feels it will please a superior.
- Lacks a substantial financial plan in place to be able to pay more in order to make more later on (short sighted).

To further understand these four types of buying motivations, consider shopping for an engagement ring. A people centric buyer may buy their ring from a local jeweler they've known for years. A process centric buyer who does most of their shopping online may buy their ring on the web (selecting their preferences and having it arrive on their doorstep). A product centric buyer may seek out a reputable brand name, such as Tiffany and Co., wanting their ring to be in the turquoise box with the company logo. Finally, a price centric buyer will find discount stores and websites; haggling and comparing for the best price.

So now that you are aware of the four P categories, how will you be able to place your target into one of them? And how will you find their X Factor? You will do it by asking a series of questions. (See Exercise 1)

Also, the X, in X Factor, is a variable and it can change at any given time and in any given place.

For example, you are shopping in housewares, and to you a ladle is just a ladle, therefore you chose the cheapest one. In this case you are acting to purchase by means of being price centric. However, in the same department, you buy a non-stick pan because it's Martha Stewart brand. You're probably doing this because you like Martha Stewart and what she puts into her brand. So, in the case of the pan you are being product centric. The takeaway is that the X Factor could change within the same isle of a department store, just as it could change from the medication a physician carries for the common cold to the cream they prescribe to a certain rash. This is what makes the X Factor sales model so different from current sales models. It takes into account the realistic ways in which people operate-allowing you, as a salesperson, to motivate the target into action, aka buying.

Why do People Buy You?

You sell yourself every day. Asking for a promotion, closing a sale and negotiating a raise are all about selling yourself. The person at the other end is sizing up your attributes, your contributions and your worth. You are a product and you are a brand. So just as the first step of a company is to define their goal and mission statement, as should you. Understanding yourself as a brand is the first step toward motivating others.

The biggest challenge in defining your personal brand is knowing yourself enough to determine your strengths and weaknesses. Your personal brand is how people see you, not how you see yourself. The message others are receiving from you can be disconnected from the way you want to be portrayed.

A simple and effective first step to understanding how others see your brand is to ask them. Send out an email to ten people today; five colleagues, and five personal friends. Ask: If there was a way to describe me professionally or personally how would you describe me?

There will be consistencies in the responses depending on the two groups of people you ask. However, your feedback describes your brand. The professional feedback may be hardworking, diligent, straight-to-the-point, takes leadership roles, takes direction well, etc. The personal feedback may be honest, loyal, supportive, and so on.

The reason that this exercise is important is that each day you hear from people who tell you their goals and where they see themselves in five or ten years. However, just as an employer conducts an interview, you can quickly surmise the possibility or impossibility of those goals being achieved based upon your evaluation of their personal brand.

Here is an example: A colleague says to you, "I want to be an expert in my field, I want to be sharp, and at the top of the chain in my environment." However, you see them day in and day out and their personal appearance is messy, they aren't up-to-date with what is happening in their field, and/or they lack the education or training to move-forward.

So moving forward, think of yourself as a company: you should have a goal, a mission statement and the right product (or background) to match.

What is your brand?

_____

_____

_____

_____

Where do you currently stand in terms of fulfilling your brand?

_____

_____

_____

_____

What can you do moving forward to meet the expectations of your brand?

_____

_____

_____

_____

What products are you People, Price, Process, and Product centric when buying? Why do you think that's so?

_____

_____

_____

_____

Thinking about the four P categories, when have you tried to motivate someone using the wrong P?

_____

_____

_____

_____

Chapter Two Summary

- The X Factor is the root cause of why someone purchases or says 'yes'.

- In order to find someone's X Factor you will identify which purchasing category your client or target falls under: People centric, Product centric, Process centric, or Price centric.

- The X, in X Factor, is a variable, and it can change at any given time and in any given place.

- You are your own personal brand.

CHAPTER THREE:
X FACTOR SELLING SYSTEM

*"I'm the guy who makes his number, you must be
the other guy."*

Tom La Vecchia

THE X FACTOR SELLING System is to identify the
subconscious and then stimulate and motivate into action.

The X Factor Selling System has four basic steps:

Open

Begin with a bold statement and direct question. You are setting
up a verbal agenda during the opening. You want to be clear as to
what your goal is. For example, "Hey, Amanda, I want to sell you
a car today. I know you came in and wanted to inquire about the
Honda Accord, so I'm very happy that you're interested, but before
we jump in and I show you the car, I do have some questions."

Thomas F. La Vecchia

From there you can provide a direct question.

"Is it a fashion statement? Is it something that you just want to use to get from point A to point B?"

You really want to ask direct questions so you can get directly to the core of what their motivation to purchase is.

Side Note:
Sometimes, unlike a car salesperson, you need to locate the purchaser. When pursuing a lead your goal is to find the decision-maker in order to start the selling process. There are different routes a sales rep takes: cold calls, warm calls, face-to-face interactions, etc. You must be able to identify the players of the business in order to know who is helpful and who is harmful in your pursuit to the decision-maker.

> *Be Aware:* Identify the players in every business:
>
> - **The Shot-caller** - the purchaser/the decision-maker. Some times you can get directly to this person and sometimes you need to go through another person or people.
> - **The Gatekeeper** - the person preventing you from whom you need to get to.
> - **The Influencer** - a person behind the scenes who you may get access to. He/she may have direct influence over the Shot-caller, but is not the final decision-maker.
> - **The Information Broker** - this is a person to look for. They are not the decision-maker or the influencer but they can provide you with valuable information.
> - **The Double Agent** - this is a person to look out for. This is a person in the purchaser's office that is in-line with the competitor. They may draw information from you and give it to a competitor. They may also provide you with false information.

Identify

Find and uncover the X Factor (your target's motivation to purchase) by using the four P's. Let's return to the car example from Open. The salesperson has got to identify what the important factor is for Amanda when buying a car. And then dig deeper to find the root cause of purchase aka her X Factor.

The X Factor process is all about understanding what exactly is leading your target to purchase so that you can not only close the sale, but are able to do so without exhausting yourself (pitching things to potential buyers blindly until you maybe hit their X Factor). When a sale is done this way it fulfills your clients true needs (typically subconscious) and therefore keeps the door open for future sales and referrals.

So let's say after your opening statement and direct question Amanda at the dealership says, "I really don't want to buy the Honda Accord, the Civic is cheaper on gas."

Okay, now she wants to purchase the Civic, which is fantastic, but it's not about the Civic, it's what's important to her. It's not about buying the Civic or the Accord, it's about buying a car, and buying the right car. And now, based on her answer, she is describing herself as price centric and her root cause is a concern over gas mileage; she feels the cheapest option for her is buying a car that gets the most miles per gallon.

However, even when asking the right questions, you are likely to get some false responses from your target. This is because many people do not know why they buy. You can assume that the potential buyers' answer to your direct question is false if there is not a close of the deal. This is okay, and it will happen. From this point, you can loop around the question process until the X Factor is truly found.

Thomas F. La Vecchia

The reason why this process requires training is because you really need to ask the right questions in order to get to the right answer. This is usually accomplished through continuous role play and various situational examples. (See Exercise 2)

So Amanda is not closing on the Civic, and let's say it has the best gas mileage in the lot; well then her motivating factor was false. So you will ask more questions: "Is it the style of the Civic that's not right for you?"

The target may come back with something they dislike about the Civics' size or body type. Okay, well now you can conclude that what is more important to Amanda than gas millage (price) is style (product). What is truly driving her to purchase is the look of the car.

My personal experience has been that customers often lie to sales representatives for various reasons: customers may lie in order to be non-confrontational, they do not know their subconscious X Factor, or they don't like you or the products that you represent. With the X Factor Selling System, you need to identify the true motivation as to why they do what they do.

Stimulate

Motivate the X Factor and gain alignment. Now that you are able to place your client or target into one of the P categories and have found their root cause of purchase, you will be able to motivate them into action.

For example, you find out on a particular sales call, someone is purchasing their material from a company because they have a great rapport with one of their representatives. Okay, well now you have established that this person is People Centric. The root cause could be a number of things: they have a lack of friendships, they like to feel important, they feel they can trust the product because they trust the rep, etc.

Here you can utilize that information in a number of ways to motivate the target to purchase:

- You may save time by not exhausting yourself finding a cheaper price, because to them it is the relationship between them and the rep that is important. So you continue on the sales call by letting them know that you can have a great rapport with them as well and proceed with the sale via their X Factor.

OR

- You can assume that to him or her, price, process or product is not something that they've had a strong focus on and use that to your advantage. You can show the purchaser that you can also have that rapport with them- as well as show them how your product is cheaper, a better brand, easier to use, etc. Therefore you have fulfilled their X Factor and have brought to their attention other factors that they have been overlooking.

Moreover, it is not simply finding and motivating someone's call to action. You must also develop an alignment to what your goal is, so that at the time of closing the deal both of your needs will be handled.

> ### *Alignment is Key**
>
> Always align their agenda with your agenda. You are looking to satisfy a customer's X Factor but to also meet your needs in order to make this process successful. The goal is to achieve mutual success through increased partnership. Once you have established which centrist they are and their X Factor, you will use this information to make a sale that benefits both them and you. In the opening you have stated what your goal is, now that you have found out a customer's X Factor you can work to gain alignment. Later in this chapter you will see an example of this with 'The Beer Salesman". Also, in Chapter Five: Marketing for the X Factor, you will learn how to present your product to gain alignment.

You will be stimulating your targets X Factor and work to gain alignment. You will find that you will have a sustainable coalition of both of your goals at the close of the sale when using this process.

Close

End with a call to action. The call to action could be a sale or one step closer, but whatever the verbal agenda, it will be a close or lead to a close. A sales call may end with a lunch date, but it will enable you to get closer to making the deal.

For example: "Yes, I can understand why you feel a sense of loyalty to your current rep. I also pride myself on my outstanding relationships with my clients. Maybe we can set-up a time and place to discuss my product over lunch. How does Thursday at 3 p.m. work for you?"

In order to make sure that both of your agendas are aligned, your closing should mirror your opening statement. All openings may not mirror the closing exactly, but you will have met both of your needs through alignment so that you have accomplished or exceeded the goals you had when you opened.

Since you have already stated what you are looking for in the beginning (your Opening), you are not waiting until the end of the interaction to present your offer-therefore the close is no longer the hardest part of the sale.

Here are a few different types of closes:

Direct Close - "Will you buy X units?"

Indirect Close - "What would you like to see in order to purchase 45 units?"

Assumptive Close - Assuming this is done, or assuming this happens, the target will purchase. "So assuming I can get the price down to ten percent less, will you purchase 45 units?" However it is more than just a verbal agreement. A true assumptive close will entail obtaining a signature or acquiring an address or phone number. This is basically a close, pending the adjustment that was agreed upon.

Trial Close - "If I give you five units for free, and you trial the product and like it, will you purchase?"

Next Step Close - "So you are trying the product for a week, next week can I come in and see if you will purchase?"

Major/Minor Close - This is very similar to a trial close, but it ups the need. "You can certainly agree that product X is the best solution to your problem. Therefore it will be a major solution to your business."

Challenge Close - This dares the customer to take action. "I understand it's difficult to make a decision and I know you're on the fence but..." or "I know it's difficult to change your life (or habit) however you need to make a move."

Negative Close - This is stressing the disadvantage of failing to act or not taking action now. This is done by explaining that if the customer does nothing, the problem will still exist and it may get worse. You may say, "The 20 percent discount will end tomorrow and will cost you X amount of dollars more if you don't act now."

Emotional Close - This is playing to someone's emotions. I'm sure you've been told by a stylist in a clothing store "That dress looks great on you! Everyone will be so jealous." Or maybe someone has said "Don't you want to make more money to put your kids through college?"

Ben Franklin Close - This is comparing the good and the bad, the pros and the cons. "Let's look at the pros and cons and then have you decide. If you go ahead and buy today you will get the 20 percent discount and the $10,000 rebate. If you don't buy today, you'll go on to fight another day, but it would be more expensive to buy it later." This is a diplomatic approach, going through what is important, and will usually focus on cost.

Worst Case/Best Case Close - "What's the worst thing that could happen if you make this purchase? If it doesn't work out you can send it back and it costs you nothing. What's the best thing that can happen? You go with this product, it works, you make let's say 40 percent more, which is the most likely scenario, and if not you can always return it."

Take Away Close - If a product is of a higher price due to a high demand special feature, you can offer to remove that feature to lower the price. This pushes the customer to purchase because they would not want a lower price if it means losing the component they desire.

With the X Factor model you will get to the close and be able to employ one of the aforementioned types of closes.

Example of a Sale Using the X Factor Selling System

"The Beer Salesman"

(This is a sophomoric example, merely to demonstrate a sale using the X Factor Selling System from start to finish)

Goal: A beer salesman must sell 45 units of Heineken to a local bar.

Salesperson: "I'm here today to sell you 45 units of Heineken. But, before I do, I would like to ask you some questions. When buying your beer what do you look for?"
[Opening statement and verbal agenda as well as direct question]

Bar Manager: "Well, to be honest, I think all beers are the same and I like to buy the cheapest beer."
[Price centric, and digging deeper it is because the they feel all beers are the same]

Salesperson: "Well I can see how you might think that. But have you ever tried imported beer?"
[In order to align goals (knowing your price cannot come down to meet your needs) you must disprove his X Factor (that all beers are the same) to steer him away from price and toward another P category.]

Bar Manager: "No I haven't."

Salesperson: "Is taste important to you?"

Bar Manager: "Well actually it is."

Salesperson: "Well I understand you think all beer is the same, but would you like to try a Heineken? I have a nice cold one here."

Bar Manager: "Wow, that's really good."
[Creating a brand loyalty, aka Product loyalty]

Salesperson: "See, so now we can at least agree that all beer does not taste the same."
[Gaining alignment]

Bar Manager: "Absolutely, this tastes a lot better."

Salesperson: "And this is only about, if you buy in bulk, which is 45 units, it's only about 20 percent more than what you're currently spending. It's probably worth it, I would think, and you tell me what you think, for a better tasting beer. And if you think all beers taste the same, than this is better than all beers, and a person like you should be selling premium beer. Can we go ahead and close you on those 45 units?"
[Ending with a call to action that satisfies both of your needs]

It is important to remember that with using the X Factor Selling System you can influence your target to spend more or less. It is not about simply finding a person's X Factor and then satisfying it despite all costs. You have to fulfill your goals as a salesperson as well.

Finding the X Factor is about figuring out why a person is purchasing, and if your goals meet right from the start that's great (i.e. your product is less expensive and they are price centric). However, such as in the aforementioned example, they do not, (i.e. your beer is more expensive and they are price centric) you can dig deeper to their root cause (they think all beer is the same) and show them differently; therefore motivating them to purchase based on brand (Heineken) and meet your sales goal (selling 45 units) by letting them know they will save money by buying in bulk.

How do you feel opening with your agenda (bold statement) will help you in closing the sale?

_____

_____

_____

_____

How might stimulating someone's motivating factor be more beneficial than over-coming objections?

_____

_____

_____

How could you utilize the 4 P's to get your target to spend more?

_____

_____

_____

_____

Chapter Three Summary

- The X Factor Selling System is to identify the subconscious and then stimulate and motivate into action.

- The X Factor Selling System has four basic steps: Open, Identify, Stimulate, and Close.

- You must identify the key players in every business: The Gatekeeper, The Shot-caller, The Influencer, The Information broker, and The Double agent.

- Alignment is key: You are looking to satisfy a customer's X Factor while also meeting *your* needs in order to make this process successful.

- There are many different types of closes, yet they should all close the deal or lead to closing the deal.

CHAPTER FOUR: ANYONE CAN BE A SALESPERSON

"The best way to predict the future is create it"

Abe Lincoln

I'VE BEEN TOLD MY entire life that I am a natural salesperson. But even with natural skill, the right nurturing is still needed to be successful. And with the right nurturing, anyone, at any time, can sell. Whether we like it or not we are always selling: Negotiating with a spouse whether we can make it to a poker game, getting your 2-year-old potty trained, or working out who gets to sit in the front seat for a long trip with friends. So the question is not can we sell, but is the clear direction in place to become a successful sales representative?

Sun Tzu, the great war theorist, philosopher and general, was sitting with the King of Wu. Wu was at war and was greatly outnumbered-by nearly 10 to 1. Sun Tzu and the King decide to go for a walk, and as they are walking, the king discloses his worries and admits that he can never win this war.

Thomas F. La Vecchia

Sun Tzu thinks for a moment and tells the King, that actually, he can. The philosopher tells the King, "You need more soldiers and a better strategy." To that the King replies that he does not have any more soldiers. Sun Tzu says, "Come with me."

The two reach the court, where the concubines are sitting around, giggling with aloof enjoyment. The concubines were women who were used to living a life of opulence as members of the King's court. Sun Tzu says to the King, "I can make them soldiers," pointing to the gaggle of women. This statement forces a chuckle out of the King, as he explains they are concubines and asks "What would they know?"

Sun Tzu proceeds to line up the girls into two groups-Group A and Group B-and while doing so he appoints one of the girls as a leader for each side. Sun Tzu then lays a sword in front of each of the appointed team leaders and says, "At the sound of the drums I want you two to fight."

The girls begin to giggle, in the same aloof manner as before, and look around at one another and the King. Neither leader picks up the sword. At this, Sun Tzu exclaims, "Maybe I wasn't clear. My order and my message are to fight at the sound of the drum." The philosopher then picks up a sword and decapitates the leader of Group A and Group B, in front of the other girls. He then proceeds to pick another leader of Group A and B, and shouts, "Fight at the sound of the drums!"

The girls pick up the swords and begin to battle one another, and it is at this point that they had become soldiers.

With Sun Tzu's clear direction and his ability to utilize the concubines, the King won the war through an expansive and disciplined army.[1]

The lesson of this story is: when the direction is not clear it is the fault of the general, but when the direction is clear, it is the fault of the subordinate. Anyone can be a soldier, when they have clear direction. Similarly, anyone can be a salesperson when given the clear direction along with the teachings of the X Factor Selling System.

The X Factor Selling System is a process; the clear direction needed to form a successful salesperson. So, an important factor in your success is having the right process. If you are at a company that has you reading scripts to customers in order to achieve a sale, or has you trying to reach nonsensical objectives, then I highly recommend that you present the X Factor Selling System to your employer.

---

[1] Tzu, *The Art of War*

Advantages of X Factor Selling Over Other Sales Methods

<u>Traditional Selling</u>: This process alters its approach based on the depth and breadth of the sale. The X Factor Selling System can be used across any spectrum of sales without needing to alter its process or approach.

<u>LAER</u>: This model's acronym stands for Listen, Acknowledge, Explore and Respond. Its goal is to teach you to be a better listener but it doesn't prepare you for changes in behavior from your target.

<u>Objection Handling</u>: This process achieves gaining short term agreement, but it does not establish any real alignment. By simply giving a customer what they want (without aligning your goals as well) you are not helping yourself as a salesperson. Simply pleasing the target this way does not produce long term success for either the buyer or the salesperson. A key aspect of X Factor Selling is the alignment of goals in order to achieve mutual success.

<u>Selling by fitting into a buyer's personality/type</u>: This process gains a salesperson entrance, but then what? Our sales system does not require either the buyer or the salesperson to fit into a mold, it is about motivating what is already in place.

<u>Features and Benefits</u>: This model is not a process as it is a marketing pitch. Using this as a sales approach is one-dimensional.

What makes The X Factor Selling System so adaptable and successful is that, in order for it to work, buyers and salespeople are not forced to fit into a mold. It is simply motivating what is already in place. Many current models or processes have employees trying to reach objectives that they do not have the right motivation to reach. Or, they are trying to push a product toward buyers that do not understand why they need it. The right process is the key to success.

It is all About Having the Right Process

"Well That's Refreshing"- By Dan Caruso

During a time of lay-offs, I moved down to a sales position at another company. I was told that this company was a recruiting firm and that I would be matching up people based on their skills to companies that were hiring. When I got there they stuck me in a room making cold calls to companies; feeling out who was hiring or not. They misled me about what the job actually was. They gave me a script, in which I had to stick to verbatim. One that made little, if any, sense and my boss sat next to me all day with a tape recorder. They had me say things to these hiring managers that anyone in their right mind would hang-up on. As people hung-up on me, I was instructed to call them back. One of the scripts I was instructed to read ran something like this: "I have just recruited a very talented developer. I am just wondering where you could find use of him in your company." The person we were referring to did not actually exist, it was just said to see if they were hiring. Now, if the hiring manger said, "We're not hiring," we were instructed to say 'Well that's refreshing to hear, what would you attribute your low turnover to?" Why is that refreshing to hear?! To this day I do not understand what the goal was of the call, given the scripts we had to follow. And we were given no training on what to say past certain lines. For example one day a hiring manager called me out on the lie and insisted I fax over the resume of this fictitious person that was looking for a job. At which point I broke out sweating with my boss standing over my shoulder. *(con't pg. 30)*

"Well That's Refreshing"- By Dan Caruso (con't from pg. 29)

Another script involved me getting the hiring manager on the phone and saying the following:

Me: 'Is this the hiring manager?'

HM: 'Yes it is, who are you?'

Me: 'That's not important, well get to that, I was actually talking to somebody the other day and they were talking about you.'

HM: 'Wait a minute. Talking about me, for what?'

Me: 'Well I can't tell you who but I can tell you why.'

HM: 'What are you talking about?!! You just called me, you're a stranger, your telling me somebody was talking about me, you won't tell me who but you'll tell me why?'

Me: 'Well yeah, it has to do with why I'm calling you today.

HM: 'Well I don't understand' [SLAMS DOWN PHONE]

Now following this my boss would instruct me to call them back! Not only that, but she would call me into her office and play back the tapes of me failing-using the scripts that we had to strictly follow. I told my boss I can't keep doing this to people, I am just completely lying and these scripts sound more like prank phone calls.

You had to call one hundred people a day and you had to find those one hundred companies on your own time. After a week, you just couldn't find anymore…they had to be in a certain state, and this and that.

The failure of this company's process was a number of things. But most importantly, it was in the scripts that they had us strictly follow. They made their employees be someone that they are not, and I think that most professionals are smarter than that and they see through it.

When I do seminars, I ask people, "Who here cooks?" and I ask them to raise-up their hands. Maybe about half of the people raise their hands. Then I ask, "Who here likes to make hamburgers?" Typically now about 75 percent of the people have their hands raised. Then I ask "Well how many people can make a better hamburger than McDonalds?" Now nearly the entire room has their hand raised. Then I say, "Okay, keep your hand up if your answer is Yes…How many people here can sell more hamburgers than McDonalds?" Their hands go right down. Why? Because McDonalds is not selling hamburgers, they are selling a process. Therefore you need to have the right process in place in order to be successful.

There are many aspects of sales, inside sales, outside sales, behind the counter sales, and the list goes on. Those who are uncomfortable with face-to-face interactions or cold calling, but have strong knowledge of how to sell and how to motivate a team, can find themselves successful in teaching-such as a Sales Manager or Leader.

It isn't that people aren't natural salespeople or that they don't like to sell; it's that people just don't like to hear "No". People in general don't like to be shot down. It's just a fact of life. But if you follow this model it will facilitate better discussions because you will be asking better questions in order to meet your and their goals.

People think selling is persuading people to do something that they don't want to do. The goal of a sale is to find out what motivates someone, identify any possible deficits or needs, get them to agree to that deficit or need, and work to meet a goal to correct it.

The X Factor process teaches you to find out what motivates someone, and from there you can stimulate an action that both satisfies your needs as well as the other persons.

Which unsuccessful processes have you used? What made them unsuccessful?

_____

_____

_____

_____

What would you like to get out of a selling process (sustainable results, easiness, etc.)?

_____

_____

_____

_____

How will you use the 4-step process of the X Factor Selling System to bring you success?

_____

_____

_____

_____

Chapter Four Summary

- With clear direction anyone can be a salesperson.

- The right process is the key to success.

- What makes the X Factor Selling System so adaptable and successful is that, in order for it to work, buyers and salespeople are not forced to fit into a mold.

- There are advantages of X Factor Selling over other sales methods.

CHAPTER FIVE: MARKETING FOR THE X FACTOR

"Marketing is too important to be left to the marketing department."

David Packard

MARKETING FOR THE X Factor means to present your product in a way that stimulates someone's motivating factor. The way a product is presented can have a large influence on how your potential buyer feels about a product and *which* product.

During the purchasing process, marketing for the X Factor can help to sway a buyer into making a decision that will meet an alignment of goals.

As with the sales portion of the method, in order to successfully market your product via the X Factor Selling System, you need to ask your customers the right questions. So prior to the advent of your marketing and branding campaign, it's critical for your customers to truthfully give feedback to the attributes of your product. Focus groups, surveys, and sampling trials can all help you to understand how the end user relates to your product.

From there, as you begin to identity who your target customers are, you can begin to understand their common X Factor. Before getting into strategy, mastering the six key selling channels to your customers is essential:

1. Your sales team; are they trained not only in the attributes of the product but on a superior selling process?
2. Advertising (print, billboard, etc.)
3. Public relations: is your product being positioned correctly?
4. Internet (websites/landing pages, email, search engine optimization, goggle ads).
5. Loyalty/referral program for existing customers
6. Customer service team: although they don't necessarily sell the product, a well-oiled customer service team is critical to customer retention

More often than not we are bombarded with ads that are ineffective because they do not grasp our attention, let alone stimulate our X Factor.

To keep it simple, any advertisement should have three critical components:

- An attention grabbing headline
- Features and benefits of the product that are important to that customer that is seeing or viewing the ad
- The most critical is a call to action. For example, an X Factor advertisement for a sales seminar may read something like this:

Do You Want To Increase Sales? Read Below
Before Your Competitor Does!
The X Factor Selling System is a proven model that will turn
your C players into A players, guide your sales team into truly
understanding their customer's needs, and help your sales team
reach their greatest potential!

Next seminar is on X DATE, call NOW as you will receive 20%
off by X Date, space is limited!

Aside from advertising, there are various strategies in terms of
pricing and marketing your product. The following are two types
of marketing strategies. These strategies can be utilized within the
X Factor Selling System. *(See Exercise 3)*

Decoy Marketing

The first marketing strategy we will look at is called **decoy
marketing**. Let's imagine you are selling watches. There are two
watches on display for your buyer. The first watch, Watch A, is
priced at $220, it's a great watch for someone on a budget, serves
the purpose and works great. The second watch, Watch B, is a little
bit better, priced at $575, and has more bells and whistles (let's say
it can tell the time in Norway).

Now by showcasing these two watches let's say 50 percent buy Watch A and 50 percent buy Watch B. Therefore, on each sale where someone chooses Watch A, you lose $355. Selling Watch B more often than Watch A would be great for your business. So how might you do this?

Let's place a third watch into the display, Watch C; a decoy watch.

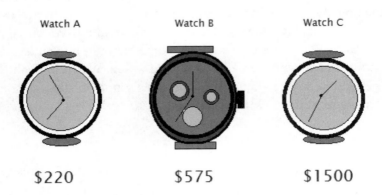

By showcasing Watch C (that looks similar to Watch A, but priced exponentially higher) the buyer's eyes are more likely to be drawn toward the middle, at Watch B.

Now Watch C is probably from the back and is probably not even sold, because it looks just like Watch A, so why would someone pay $1,280 extra? By adding a decoy you are influencing the buyer to look where you want them to look, and it can enable a salesperson to make a product appear more desirable. Using all three watches in the display, you are forcing a buyer's eyes to look at the right, look to the left, and bounce back to the middle. This is a marketing strategy that is used in a number of ways and in numerous arenas.

How can you apply this to X Factor Selling? Decoy marketing can be used to muddy a target's X Factor. Let's say your buyer says, "I want to buy the cheapest watch because I'm focused on purely functionality." Therefore, given the first display, they choose to purchase Watch A. However by using decoy marketing and adding Watch C, they may perceive Watch B to be a better value.

Aura of Legitimacy

The next marketing strategy is the aura of legitimacy. Presenting an aura of legitimacy is to make something seem more valuable than it is in order to get someone to purchase or take action. An example of this method could be seen through platinum selling artists. Notable celebrities have broken into the top selling charts by giving away albums for free and logging them as sales. By doing this they are presenting an aura of legitimacy of high sales numbers. By creating a platform that looks successful, others become more intrigued to buy. So, by others seeing a record has high sales, they begin to jump on the bandwagon and purchase.

Another example of aura of legitimacy is half price drinks on a Wednesday. Now normally, let's say, the mixed drinks at a bar-restaurant are roughly $14. So you go on a Wednesday for the $7 drinks and you feel that you are getting a deal. However the normal $14 drink price is marketed up so high that the bar is making an 80 percent profit on your drinks; the $7 they are charging on a Wednesday is merely matching what most of the bar-restaurants on the block charge daily. But you go to that bar on a Wednesday because you feel you are getting a deal.

Presenting an aura of legitimacy is something that every salesperson should understand. Just as you can present an aura of legitimacy to your customer, they can present an aura of legitimacy to you, or your competition can present this to your customers. Avoiding this ploy is done by looking to see what the price is relative to the market, what the sellers' or buyers' strategy is, and deciding if it is legitimate.

As previously discussed, when finding someone's X Factor a target may give untruthful answers because most people do not know why they buy. However giving an untruthful answer intentionally is presenting an aura of legitimacy. When a customer is intentionally feeding you false information (presenting an aura of legitimacy) you will treat it the same way as mentioned before and loop around the question process. For example a customer says, "Oh I can't do it because we're out of budget." Or "I can't buy anything because my boss says." They are telling you they cannot do A, B, and C because of all of these areas of "legitimacy." So you must identify what is legitimate and what is not. So beware of the aura of legitimacy but seek true legitimacy in your business deals.

The Car Salesman - By Dan Caruso

Years ago, I worked as a car salesman. As I am sure most of you know, there are many 'tricks of the trade' that go on during the selling process when negotiating the price of a car. Well, during my time as a sales manager I have seen it all. Ever wonder what happens when a salesman leaves you at the desk to 'go back and talk to the manager about lowering the price'? As you are left sitting there, mulling over a number of things, anxiously awaiting their return, what are they actually doing back there?! Eating. Chatting about you (unrelated to the sale). Napping. You name it-they're doing possibly anything or everything but talking numbers with their boss. And maybe, if they actually do get around to talking price, it is in the last minute of the twenty minutes that they have left you alone. Of course, when they return they will continue on with either, 'okay so we can do this' or 'he says we really can't come down on price, or 'any lower and we are losing money.' So why do salesman do this? Aura of legitimacy. By the salesman going back to seemingly negotiate the price for you with a higher-up, their response holds an elevated authenticity and it makes you feel more important that they did so.

Pricing Your Product

Now let's take a moment to touch on pricing your product. Pricing crosses lines between all four P's and therefore is important to understand. With X Factor Selling you need to decide if price is important not assume price is important during the negotiation process. You will identify what is important to the customer and then identify your pricing strategy.

For example, a common complaint amongst salespeople is, "This guy is such a jerk! I've bent over backwards to get him the best price and he still hasn't allowed me to close the deal." With X Factor Selling, you will know which P category your target falls under (and their X Factor) and they may be Product or Process centric, therefore being offered a lower price will not motivate their X Factor and cause them to act.

Using the four P's and choosing a pricing strategy accordingly is how we as salespeople can get a target to spend more or less to gain an alignment of goals.

Objection Handling: Not Always About Price

*Andy and *Joe were sales reps for a company that sold a product that was newer to the market. Andy took the route of finding out what motivated his customers and Joe was more of a price guy; getting people to buy based on price so they could make more money. They only had ten trial units each with the goal of selling 400 units each for retail. Their objective was to get buyers to try this product so that they would use it on a regular basis. Both strategies were successful in the beginning.

Now when the 10 units increased to unlimited units of trial basis, they took two dramatically different routes. Andy took his resources, which again were sample units, and decided to train and educate the customers, as well as evaluate with the customers. Andy did not lower his price in any way but focused on getting his clients to really appreciate the product, love the product and understand the product for what it was. Sure he gave an occasional free-bee out here and there, but he focused on the strategy of getting them more comfortable.

Joe took the opposite route. His strategy was 'If you love this product, buy 10 and I'll give you 2', to lower the price to make them more money. But then competition started coming in and it became buy 10, get 3. Buy 10, get 4. It got to the point that some people were buying 10 and getting 10; lowering Joe's average price. Now maybe, some of Joe's customers were making more than Andy's customers, but Andy's customers believed in the product and they shared an alignment of goals.

Andy beat Joe that year, simply because he focused on getting his customers to love the product. Joe became the 'price leader' and as soon as the next cheapest thing came along he lost that business overnight. Maybe some customers are about price, or price centric, but it is not always about simply coming in at a lower cost.

Thomas F. La Vecchia

However, the price of your product relative to the market is important. You must always recognize who you are aiming to sell to overall and know what types of products are already available to gain entry into the market.

When pricing a product you must consider three factors:

Skimming or Premium Pricing - This means to charge the highest possible price; as your product justifies (or perceives to justify) a higher price or premium.

Parity Pricing - This type of pricing falls in the middle of the marketplace in order to gain adequate market share while pricing into a group that is often crowded.

Penetration Pricing - This is setting the lowest possible price; most of the time it will be the lowest price in the market. This is done to gain market share through bargain basement pricing. With this pricing strategy you will gain quick access to the market, but it may cut into your margins and also, possibly, have a negative effect on your brand.

In what situations could you use decoy marketing?

_____

_____

_____

_____

How will you change your strategy when it comes to knowing it's not always about price?

_____

_____

_____

_____

Has someone ever presented you with an aura of legitimacy? If so, how could you have handled the situation better?

_____

_____

_____

_____

Chapter Five Summary

- Before getting into strategy, mastering the six key selling channels to your customers is essential.

- To keep it simple, any advertisement should have three critical components.

- Decoy marketing is a strategy used to increase sales.

- Understanding the aura of legitimacy can help to avoid ploys and in seeking truthful business deals.

- With X Factor Selling you need to decide *if* price is important not assume price is important during the negotiation process. You will identify what is important to the customer and *then* identify your pricing strategy.

CHAPTER SIX: INSIDE THE MIND OF A SALES MANAGER

"If one does not know to which port one is sailing, no wind is favorable."

Lucius Annaeus Seneca

THIS CHAPTER WILL PROVIDE insight into the needs and wants of a sales manager. The goal is to understand what your supervisor's X Factor is. Typically, sales managers toe the company line. They want to look good, to make money off of your efforts, and be promoted. In order to do these things, a manager looks to take certain steps.

First, it is critical that they have the right people in place. Having the right people on their team is crucial. Looking back to the story of Sun Tzu, clear direction is everything; however they want the right people to execute it. I would rather have a team of the right people without direction, than the wrong people with direction, because they may not be able to execute it. And yes, anyone can be a salesperson given the right training, but the right people are those with the drive and initiative and positive thinking. You will learn how to ensure you are the right person for the team, and how to stay on the team.

Thomas F. La Vecchia

Sales Leaders have nearly 8-10 people under them, a Director roughly 20-200, and a CEO may have 500-5,000 people working under them. Nevertheless, they have no more than ten to fifteen direct reports. Whenever I put together a team I look and I interact and have an alignment meeting on day one with each person. I will ask each person what their X Factor is, what their goal is, and how long it will take them to get there. I will gain alignment on that and then put an action plan in place. A manager can see your demeanor, the way you act, and then look at your results and so forth.

There are three tiers or types of salespeople that a manager may have working under them. Like a traffic light, they can be categorized into Green, Yellow, and Red groups.

The Green - These are that top performers, they are engaged and love what they do. These performers are most likely given a little bit of coaching and resources, but for the most part are able to work more independently. It is obvious that you want to find yourself on the Green team. Once you are on this team, your goals should be aligned with your sales manager.

The Yellow - This team is the most critical. The Yellow will more than likely be the bulk of the team members. These team members are likely to air more on the side of: Well I could do better, and they're not. Or they want to do better, and they don't know how. Skill versus will. These team members are ambivalent and they are just making their numbers or slightly under their number. They're engagement level is not high or they are engaged but don't know how to increase their sales. If you are in the Yellow you need to seek out what is missing for you to be a part of the Green. If it is the will that you are missing then sit down with your manager and discuss incentives. If it is the skill you need to work on then ask for training and resources to fulfill your developmental needs.

48

The Red - You will recognize these people as the rebel-rousers; calling the rest of the team after conference calls, trying to derail the company at all costs. Spotting a Red team member is usually obvious. They may be performing in the short-run, but not in the long-run. These team members are the cancer in the group. If you find yourself on the Red team than you should seriously consider leaving the current company you are working for-whether you leave or they ask you to leave- you do not have a long standing career where you are. Also, a Red team member at one company could be a Green team member at another, so seriously consider your position.

In a manager's mind, the Yellow and Red team members are often the influencers of the group, and may pull someone down from Green or Yellow. More likely than not, it is the Red team members that may pull down the middle.

A team may have two or three people in Green, five people in Yellow, and two or three in Red. The key job of a sales leader is to move the middle. A manager's job is to Hire, Train, Sell, and Repeat. With the Yellow team members they may have an open, frank, and candid clarifying discussion. I would ask questions to my Yellow team members such as: *What are you looking to do? What are your expectations?* And say to them, *Here are my expectations*, and gain alignment and hold them to that alignment. In my experience, if a Yellow team member falls out of alignment, than they will most likely fall into the Red.

Something else to consider is know what motivates you. (See Exercise 4) Your sales leader and/or manager want to see you perform and succeed. However, you may be lacking the motivation you need to be successful. Whether be better incentives, more recognition, or better training, let your manager know what will push you to reach and exceed your numbers.

Recognition - Know What Motivates You

During my time with a team that I managed, I sat down with one of the team members, *Joe, early on to work to gain alignment. One of the first things he said was that he had three children, and one was very sick. The child had a form of bone cancer. Joe said he was just looking to make more money. "I am about money, I am looking to make money," he said. So through my position as manager I got him a raise and worked on getting him resources to better do his job. Directly, or indirectly, I put a lot more money in his pocket by doing so. So some time later on, I did a full day seminar. At the end I said, 'Here are the top performers, here is what is going on,' and I gave recognition to two or three members of my team. After the seminar was over, Joe approached me and said, "Hey Tom, how come you didn't recognize me? I'm one of your top performers." My response to him was, "I asked you at the beginning what was important to you. And you said money. I put at least twenty thousand more in your pocket this year. You didn't come to me and say recognition was important." So he looked at me and said, "You're right. But you know what Tom? I didn't want to admit this, but recognition is also important to me."

My point being, know what really motivates you.

Currently at your place of business do you feel that you are in the Red, Yellow, or Green team?

_____

_____

_____

_____

How would gaining alignment with your superior help push you further into the Green team? What would you ask for alignment on?

_____

_____

_____

_____

What motivates you?

_____

_____

_____

_____

Chapter Six Summary

- There are three tiers or types of salespeople that a manager may have working under them. Like a traffic light, they can be categorized into Green, Yellow, and Red groups.

- A manager's job is to Hire, Train, Sell, and Repeat.

- The relationship between a rep and a sales manager is key-know your manager's X Factor, gain alignment, and achieve mutual success.

- Know what motivates you.

CHAPTER SEVEN: SUCCESS IN SALES CALLS FOR PASSION

You can't feign passion...

Unknown

Passion (noun)

- intense, driving, or overmastering feeling or conviction

- a strong liking or desire for or devotion to some activity, object, or concept

- an object of desire or deep interest[2]

In this book we will teach you how to sell, however we cannot install passion. Therefore it is critical to be passionate about your sales career.

Whenever I think about passion I think about Babe Ruth, and most likely not for the reason you'd think.

---

[2] *Merriam-Webster's Dictionary, "passion."*

In the early 1900s, Babe Ruth was a star player for the Boston Red Sox, where he started out as a pitcher, but because he was such a great hitter, he graduated to the outfield. Ruth was sold to the New York Yankees for, at the time, a very large sum. This trade was in all probability the worst thing to ever happen to the Red Sox and the best thing to ever happen to the Yankees franchise. After all, the original Yankee stadium was "the house that Ruth built."

Now, the owner of the Red Sox at the time, Harry Herbert Frazee, sold Ruth to the Yankees not to dump the money back into the Red Sox, but to use the money to fund a musical theater company.

Boston suffered for the next seventy or eighty years. They called it the "Curse of the Bambino," and it caused a lot of heartache in the Boston area- and a lot of fanfare for New York City.

The reason why I look to this story when I think about passion is to remind myself to work within my passion. Frazee wasn't passionate about baseball; he took that money and put it into his side project- his real passion-and caused tremendous heartache for the Boston area baseball fans for decades to come.

When it comes to achieving success you must be honest with yourself: Know what *your* X Factor is and honestly decide where you should be applying this process. As a result you will be presenting the best results when measuring your success.

As was mentioned in *Inside the Mind of a Sales Manager*, a sales team needs to have the right people in place. But it does not have to be solely a manager's job to make sure that you are at the right company. It should be a decision that you take into your own hands. It is critical for you to take control of your own future and not have others determine it for you. Only you can determine what you consider to be success, and as far as I am concerned, passion is the linchpin.

'Chi Dorme non piglia pesch'
He who sleeps doesn't catch fishes.

There is a story my mother often tells (it sounds better in Italian), that goes back nearly thirty years ago to when I was a kid. A woman in our neighborhood lost her cat. At the time it was difficult to post flyers with pictures on them, so you had to use a description. On the flyer the woman wrote the cat's name and stated that there was a five dollar reward for finding her cat. So, I scoured the neighborhood and found a cat and knocked on the woman's door. The woman looked at the cat I brought to her and said, "That's not my cat." So I continued to search the neighborhood and each time I brought her a new cat she said, "That's not my cat." And so, after the fifth cat, the woman said, "Listen kid, I appreciate your effort. Here's five dollars. Thank you, but don't worry about my cat."

My point being, although I didn't reach my end goal, I worked my butt off to get there, and a lot of the time people respect that. In sales it's all about hitting the number, it's all about making money, but you can't do it unless you have the work ethic…and you're willing to at least *look* for the cat.

As social beings it is very important for us to be influential, especially for people in the sales profession. We are constantly selling things to our friends, convincing them to go out and see a movie we loved or to read a book that we couldn't put down, or to visit a website because they have the best prices and quality products. We tell friends to try a project we did around the house by telling them how easy it was, and how much money we saved. Without even thinking, we are making great sale points, speaking passionately, and influencing others to buy into something. Now imagine you are getting paid for that. That is what a sales representative's work day should be.

Although passion is needed to succeed in the long run – it could be seen as a luxury to be selling an outstanding product that excites you for the time being.

A large part of having passion is believing in the product you sell – however, in the situation of being obligated to sell a certain product, or in a temporary situation, sometimes selling something that doesn't excite you happens.

So, as you continue to look onward for your choice sales position, for now you must sell that not-so-hot product to stay afloat. Here are some tips to exercise in order to succeed when the passion just isn't there.

1. **Make yourself process centric.**

   My sales philosophy states the 4 P's of why people buy: People, Product, Process and Price. However, this philosophy can also be used as a process for you as the salesperson to take part in. Become product agnostic, emerge yourself in your selling process, therefore shifting your excitement to your process instead.

2. **Take a note from PR.**

   Public Relations is all about spinning an average story and making it sound miraculous. Be the PR person of your product! As PR people "news jack" and link an average story to current events to capture the public eye, think about how you can connect your product to current mainstream issues. So, when speaking to a company decision maker, think about what is on his/her mind and tie your product to that issue in any way you can. For example: I know many people in your position are worried about X, and my product can indirectly or directly help to solve X because of XYZ.

3. **Make a list of all of the bad attributes of your product, or where it falls short relative to the market: price, utility, etc.**

   There must be some area where it makes up for those loses: i.e.: it doesn't have the best utility but it is priced 20 percent lower. So, if that is the case, use this information to your benefit and seek leads that are price centric not product (brand, utility) centric.

4. **Finally see your current job (selling your bad product) as a resume booster.**

   Realize that you blowing out your number with a not-so-hot product will speak volumes to your sales ability. While interviewing for new positions explain how you triumphed with a bad product and ask them "I sold X product and here are my numbers. Now, imagine if I was selling *your* product that I *believe* in?"

It is frustrating when you are stuck in a position and looking for help and all you can find for "How to sell a bad product" comes back as "You don't. So, if your choice position is restrictive for the time being- you can keep looking for that new position-but in the meantime exercise this tips.

1. When have you felt passionate about convincing someone to buy/do something? How easy was it to convince them?

_____

_____

_____

_____

2. Are you currently passionate about what you sell? If no, why?

_____

_____

_____

_____

Chapter Seven Summary

- Know what *your* X Factor is and honestly decide *where* you should be applying this process to achieve the best results when measuring your success.

- It does not have to be solely a manager's job to make sure that you are at the right company.

- No one can install passion in you.

- You are solely responsible for your professional development.

CHAPTER EIGHT: MEASURING YOUR SUCCESS WITH X FACTOR

"Rule #1 is to never lose money, Rule #2 is to never forget rule number one."

Warren Buffet

WHATEVER SUCCESS LOOKS LIKE to you, there must be metrics in place to show that you've reached sustainable results.

Sales is a numbers game. If you follow the X Factor Selling System, you will not only make more money, but you will be more efficient in your approach to motivate others. Very simply, by getting to the heart of the matter more quickly you are not wasting your time on unprofitable (or unbeneficial) activity. The way to gauge your success is to set-up goals for yourself and a way to measure those goals.

The key to success is recognizing what works and what doesn't. So the first step in measuring your success is to nail down your process for success. Also, when you have an unsuccessful interaction it is just as important to know why it wasn't successful.

Thomas F. La Vecchia

Since we often measure our results via our sales numbers its extremely important that not only are we able to read our sales numbers, but to fully understand the story they are telling us. We are presenting this model to a wide audience; however the commonality of the various success standards is to be profitable.

If you're in a sales environment, very often you are defined by performance. This can lead to a roller coaster of emotions that can either boost your performance or keep you down in the dumps. The old adage is true: Motion creates emotion.

- First thing to remember is that your numbers define your performance, not you.

- However, how you perform is the direct cause of your results. In other words, the choices you make have an effect on your bottom line, hence your financial performance and very often your overall wellbeing (professionally at least).

So if you're doing great, congratulations to you and the best of success. However, performing well or not, it is important to know why you're receiving your results. Recognizing a successful process means you can repeat it in order to gain future success. Intern, recognizing an unsuccessful process means you can re-evaluate your strategy.

If you find yourself in an underperforming rut, here are some questions you should be asking yourself:

• Look in the mirror. Are you at the right company; one that suits your values and skill sets. If not, go to place that is in line with your values/beliefs.

- Are you passionate about your vocation? If you won the lottery would you stay at this job or in this industry?

- What is your strategy? Perhaps you're great at selling, but not great at targeting. Where are you getting your leads from? Are they qualified leads or pulled from the sky?

- Are you executing? Be honest with yourself. If your home at 2 p.m. on a workday in your pajamas, you're probably slacking off a bit.

After you have identified the cause of your underperformance, here are three steps to get out of your rut and build metrics to insure you've reached sustainable results:

- Set daily and weekly goals that are realistic and attainable. (See Exercise 5)

- Build your entire infrastructure around these goals so that you're in a situation that is more conducive to your success. If you're in sales, set-up a protocol to feed your pipeline with qualified leads. Or, put together your own CRM program to best manage your relationships. All efforts have to set you up for success, so dedicate the time to make it happen.

- Align Strategy with Execution: When the strategy is clear, execution becomes the strategy. Set the right goals, have qualified leads (i.e. hot targets) and be well trained on your product offering.

It's not easy to get out of a slump, especially when it sometimes seems like the world is against you. People become more sensitive to negative events when times are tough. So if you think you're a poor salesperson, then follow these steps in order to get your business back on track.

In order to know what great looks like, you need to establish your goals early on in the process, organize your infrastructure around achieving those goals, and always expect excellence.

What Success Looks Like to Me: Competitive Immunity

I had a customer that was buying roughly 300 units from me and about 200 units from the competition. I was selling the 300 units of product to a physician's office. So we were sharing nearly 50 percent market share from this particular client. So, I went in and presented a plan showing how my company's products would be more profitable for them if buying all from us. This is how: I put a plan in place to install the right people in their care facility to make sure they could move the units. I installed a solid sales process (the X Factor model) so that their employees knew how to intensely sell and move the units. Finally, I made sure that the product was properly marketed within the office. In a three-year time period I not only gained fullmarket share but this physician went from buying 300 units from us to 1500 units – a five-fold increase. His business increased from $300,000 a year in income to 1.2 million by following the X Factor model.

This was a highly successful celebrity plastic surgeon with a thriving practice. Prior to meeting with me he would deem his practice as successful by pretty much any measure. But by partnering with me, and following my sales model, he nearly quadrupled his business. So, it's always critical to evaluate and reevaluate what success looks like to you, because if he had settled at just being good he would have never aspired to be great.

If you are beginning a career in Sales as an owner (for example a retail store) or a department manager (overseeing sales numbers) it is extremely important to look at the overall message of your sales numbers.

Case Study: Measuring Retail Shipping Success

A shipping store was up 20 percent versus the previous year. However its profit was down 10 percent. Why is that, considering the extraordinary top line increase? Well this particular store shipped packages and offered various business services. Over the course of the year and the change in economy, the shift from business services (that were highly profitable) migrated toward traditional shipping services (that were much lower margin). So in retrospect this business was taking more money in, but keeping less. For me, it's not about the money you make, but the money you keep. So the solution for this business was to change their selling process by adapting the X Factor Selling System; asking a few simple questions when servicing the retail customers. By asking simple questions they were able to up-sell and cross-sell from shipping at a rate of 25 percent. For example, packaging and office supplies: which resulted in not only a 25 percent top line increase, but a 25 percent profit-increase across the board in just six months. With just a few simple questions they were able to steer sales to a better profit margin center, from shipping to business services, by tweaking their sales approach with the X Factor selling process.

So, owners and managers simply looking at top line sales would be happy with a 25 percent increase. However, while top line statements may look good, the bank account statements may not. So as I consulted for this company I realized they simply measured success by top line sales versus the previous year, as opposed to looking at a wider picture. After our initial assessment we came up with the following plan: Moving forward, this particular business would measure their success via examining the following reports on a daily basis. We kept it simple by having them review two reports on a daily basis.

- Report by profit center (sales), which included shipping, document services, etc.

- Report by sales associate (average sale transaction per sales associate).

By doing this we were able to monitor sales activity by profit center and steer sales training efforts towards the higher profit margin products; which also included sales contests for associates in order to stimulate sales in these key areas. Next we looked at the average sale per retail representative and stack ranked them from one to five (best to worst of the five employees). Therefore, we knew exactly what was selling and who was selling the most. So in this case we were able to quickly identify who was under performing and coach them in order to achieve better results, in some cases terminating those who were unable to make the cut.

So in order to know what great looks like, you need to establish your goals early on in the process, organize your infrastructure around achieving those goals, and always expect excellence. That is critical to measuring success via the X Factor Selling System.

If you are just beginning, be sure to set-up goals for yourself and put in place a way to measure those goals.

The economy is tough and people and businesses are hurting. Managers and CEO's alike are looking to cut costs; I think that's the wrong move. If sales could be increasing to existing customers and maybe new customers, they wouldn't necessarily need to cut costs. And the key to doing so is having the right metrics in place to measure that success; along with the right people and processes.

1. Describe one process that you use for repeated successful results.

_____

_____

_____

_____

2. What is your daily goal? Weekly goal?

_____

_____

_____

_____

Chapter Eight Summary

- Whatever success looks like to you, there must be metrics in place to measure that you've reached sustainable results.

- Since we often measure our results via our sales numbers, it's extremely important to fully understand the story they are telling us.

- In order to know what great looks like, you need to establish your goals early on in the process, organize your infrastructure around achieving those goals, and always expect excellence.

CHAPTER NINE: ORIGINS OF X FACTOR SELLING

"Mutual Success through increased partnership..."

X Factor Motto

THE RESULTS OF MY method for increasing sales numbers began to materialize during my experience as a team leader - for four different sales teams, whose regions spanned across different geographies, consisting of diverse products. All of which were taught (what I now call) The X Factor Selling System and showed exponential growth in sales given a six to twelve month time period.

The first sales team I managed was selling in the New York and Maine area. When I had arrived it was ranked 9th out of twelve teams, but, with my coaching, this team rose to number one. Of this particular team I was a sales rep and then was promoted to lead. Although we were getting great sales results after adopting the X Factor Selling System, I was a bull in a China shop. I was very aggressive with one rep in particular about getting his numbers up. But then I started asking questions, and using the X Factor method on him. I found out that his X Factor was trust between him and his sales leader. And although he trusted me as a peer he did not yet trust me as a leader. So, as I learned that trust was important to him, I developed trust over time so I could give him the coaching and direction he needed-and he was accepting of it. It was then I learned the importance of trust in a sales leader.

The second team, in central New Jersey, was ranked 53rd out of ninety-three teams, and rose to third place within six months of my arrival. This was the first full-time team I managed and it had a lot of challenges. One of my team members owed $25,000 to the company, due to an administrative error, and he was very sensitive about paying that money back; he believed it wasn't his fault. His salary was $100,000 a year, so he owed 25 percent of his salary. I believed he already had trust in me, but that his X Factor was the need for mentorship. He employed the X Factor model within his daily sales calls and not only paid the money he owed back, but he made 25 percent year-over-year in total salary and commission (and within three years doubled his total earnings). So here the X Factor System worked two-fold: he employed the model and I employed the model to find out what his motivating factor was (mentorship). From this I took away the importance of knowing what motivates your team. After coming up with a way to pay back the money while maintaining his yearly salary he stayed with the company and I am proud to not only call him a colleague, but a friend.

The third team located in southern New Jersey, was ranked 100th out of one-hundred and fifteen sales teams, and rose to 15th place in less than nine months. This team I managed was not only a low ranked sales team, but the previous leader failed miserably at recognizing their efforts. Although they employed the X Factor Selling System, with the majority of this team recognition was key. Think about how many times you talk to your supervisor and hear critiques as opposed to, "You're doing a good job." This team employed the X Factor System, which is great, but sometimes success can be driven by a simple and well-deserved, "Good job."

The fourth team was 11th out of eleven and after employing the X Factor method they tied for 2nd in the nation. This team's district was spread as far as the mid-west. I noticed that the challenges of this team (trust and mentorship) were very similar to that of the previous three; but the successful constant was the employment of the X Factor Selling System.

After brining these teams to success I realized I had formed a process: one that proved to be teachable, universal, and successful. After using it as a sales leader and seeing the results, I knew I had something special. I realized I was teaching my staff the *how* and not the *what*. In other words, I was teaching them a method, not giving them objectives. I took this model and then tweaked it into a fashion that can make anyone successful in sales. Not only can this method be used to create great salespeople but it can also be used throughout everyday life situations.

In considering the success of my process I not only looked into the top 10 percent of salespeople that were doing well, but also the 90 percent that were doing poorly. I had concluded that within the large percentage of failing salespeople there was lack of a deep understanding of their customers and their customers' X Factor.

And so, I had asked myself, do I continue on and manage the fifth, sixth, and seventh team? Or do I share this model with the world…

What is at the core of X Factor Selling? Truth be told, it is selfishness that truly motivates each and everything that we do. Most commonly, a salesperson is simply looking to push their product over the competition in order to meet or exceed their sales ratio. This is usually done without any regards to what is best for the customer, best for the company, and most importantly, you as a salesperson. Most sales companies typically focus on overcoming objections, which is an even bigger waste of time.

As a sales rep I've noticed that customers and salespeople are motivated by various factors. Whether it is social status, finances, recognition, etc., no customer ever did anything simply because they felt that their objection was handled. Intern, no salesperson is motivated unless they are receiving what they need in return. People act in their own self-interest. In addition, much of what motivates people into making a decision to act lies in the subconscious, many people do not know why they do what they do.

One day a gentleman was walking around the outskirts of his property and he noticed a tree that was larger amongst the others. The man found this tree to be an eyesore and thought to himself that he wanted it gone.

The next day a couple walked by the man's yard with their young child and they noticed the man was beginning to tie-up the large tree and realized he was going to cut it down.

The man and woman stopped abruptly and starred in disbelief. They then approached the man and plead, "Sir! Please don't cut down this tree! This is where me and my husband had our first kiss, and now we have a child together. We come back here on our anniversary to celebrate our love and our family. It means so much to us."

The man listened to the couple and then went about his plans to cutting down the tree; un-swayed to change his mind.

Hours later, an old man with a walking cane approached the man who persistently was working to cut down the tree. The old man approached the property owner and said, "I used to take naps under this tree, I used to come here with my wife when she was alive...look here," he said pointing to the lower trunk of the tree, "these are our initials that we carved into the bark." The old man looked deep into the axe wielding man's eyes and begged, "Please do not cut down this tree."

The landowner declared in frustration, "Please get out of my way." He continued on with his plans to chopping down the hefty tree.

The man wound-up with the axe, and struck the trunk with a "thwack!" The man felt satisfied and began to pull the axe from the tree. As soon as his sharp blade was pulled out of the trunk, however, a spurt of syrup began to slide down the trunk to the roots.

Placing down the axe, the man reached out his finger and scooped up some of the sticky sludge. He tasted the syrup and thought, how delicious!

Realizing how lucrative the maple tree was, he decided to keep the tree and use it as a source of income. He announced that anyone could come by and enjoy the tree as they pleased; it was not going anywhere now.[3]

The bottom line is that people do not act unless it is in their own self-interest. The tree was not seen as valuable to the landowner, and the objections of the passerby's did not motivate him to see it as such. Searching his property the landowner saw the tree as an eyesore and therefore hurting his property value, so he did not act to save it until he saw it as an income, therefore serving his interest.

The X Factor Selling System can lead anyone to figuring out someone's motivating factor (their X Factor) and from there motivate a target to say 'yes' and therefore act. One of the foundations of the X Factor Selling System is that in order to get someone to act you must uncover their subconscious motivating factor. So by sifting out what the great reps were doing right, constructing a process through my experience, and realizing people act when it benefits them, the X Factor Selling System was created.

---

[3] Greene and Joost, *The 48 Laws of Power*.

Chapter Nine Summary

- The X Factor Selling System materialized as a result of bringing four different sales teams to success.

- The X Factor Selling System is a process; it teaches the *how* not the *what*.

- Successful sales representatives have a deep understanding of their customer's X Factors.

- People act in their own self-interest.

CHAPTER TEN: NOT QUITE ENOUGH

"Effort only fully releases its reward after a person refuses to quit."

Napoleon Hill

LATER ON IN MY sales career I was sent back to that same care center in the South Bronx as was mentioned in Chapter One. What I had found out about this particular care center is that they were not keen on sales representatives. Frankly, the reason that they were not favorable to reps was because they felt they didn't present enough value to their patients. It was a Medicaid/Medicare setting and they felt that reps were like a leech on the healthcare system. Well, I had a sales call and goals to meet. So I went in, again, and talked to that doctor, again.

Here is what I said: "Listen, I want to provide value for your busy practice, but before I do I need to know how I can best help you." He replied with, "Well, really, you can't. I'm involved with certain access and certain products."

I found out, through questioning, using the X Factor process, that he could use our products under his strict limitations. Here is where I made a bold move, and I am not suggesting this on every call or with every customer.

I looked at the doctor and said bluntly, "I probably want to be here less than you want me here. It's about an hour from my house, it's in the South Bronx, and I can't even find parking."

He was thrown off.

So I made an agreement with him: If he steered 30 percent of the business my way, which was well above my market share at the time (which was 18 percent), that I would not come in to the center. I would leave him alone. Therefore, my value add to him was actually not being there.

We had a handshake agreement. I met his goal of leaving him alone and he met my goal of almost doubling my market share.

I went back into that care center only one time since our handshake, and it was because he dipped below 20 percent. Upon entering the clinic he saw me, and just by virtue of seeing me he said, "Hey Tom, you know what...I fell off a little, you're right for coming in here. And I don't want to see you."

I replied with, "I don't want to see you either."

He went back to his 30 percent and all was well.

So in terms of X Factor, sometimes it's not what you do, it's what you don't do. I realized that I really couldn't add a ton of value to him, and further he didn't want me pestering him.

I know it's not a fancy elaborate story on how to crack a sales goal but I was able to exceed my sales numbers by finding out that his particular X Factor was essentially not seeing me. We aligned, he achieved his treatment goals, and I exceeded my sales numbers.

1.   What do you think was done differently the second time on that Sales call that motivated the Doctor to purchase?

_____

_____

_____

_____

2.   Looking back on a situation of defeat, what could you have done differently?

_____

_____

_____

_____

CHAPTER ELEVEN: PUTTING IT All TOGETHER

MY PARENTS EMIGRATED FROM Italy in 1959. They came to this country for a better life for themselves and their children. Early on in my career I never expected that I would go into sales. I truly thought that I would just land a corporate job, make X amount per year, and just be happy that I was able to find gainful employment and provide for my family. However, innately I always knew I wanted to be more, that being said, I decided I wanted to go into sales. I didn't want my income to be determined by anyone else but me. I wanted my income to be determined off of my desire and willingness to win.

As I started to gain more experience in sales I did notice what the great reps did versus the not great reps. I said to myself, well why don't the bad reps do what the great reps do? Well truth is they don't want to. So number one, will is the most important factor, it's important to have the passion. Secondly, it's skill. Although you may have some natural skill, you need to be refined. Or you may not have the 'natural' skill and you want to succeed in sales, then you can be taught how to engage your customers in the right fashion. So that is basically the foundation for the X Factor Selling System. I've made a ton of money as a rep from employing the model, it was more innate at the time; I didn't identify it as the X Factor Selling System until I was a sales manager. As a manger I've taught this model and have more than doubled my sales representatives' income.

So my goal is pretty simple, I created the X Factor Selling System in order to inspire greatness. I want you to reach your fullest and highest potential in whatever endeavor you déicide to carry out. This is not strictly meant as just a sales model to be used by sales people; this could be used in customer service, marketing, and even with operations. Hopefully you have found this book to be meaningful and it has provided some insight on how to better connect with people by finding out what truly motivates them and aligning your goals. At the time of writing this book I am in the process of putting together a website at thesalesexpertusa.com, at which there will be multiple online resources as well as seminars to be announced. I wish you the best of luck and hopefully you have enjoyed the X Factor Selling System.

AFTERWORD

By John Troland,
Executive Producer of Business Beat Live

One might wonder how the Executive Producer and host of the 18 year airing TV show might benefit from Tom La Vecchia's book "The X Factor Selling System." It benefits both myself and my clients in my non-TV business ventures and as it would for any salesperson wishing to substantially increase their sales based income.

A great sales person does not substantially increase their income by luck or happenstance. The great ones do so by utilizing a system. While one could certainly find other so called "systems" available, the X Factor Selling System is the system for ultimate sales success. It is unique in that it seeks to identify the subconscious and then stimulate and motivate a customer into action (making a buying decision).

This book states that anyone can be a salesperson given the right process and training...while you can teach skill, the reader must have the will and passion to carry it out."

My advice is to adopt and utilize the X Factor Selling System, combined with your will and passion, and the net result will be you becoming a master of selling.

I am a tax accountant, business plan writer and small business consultant outside of the television world. In each of those endeavors invariably I need to "sell a client" on both the value of my services and the greater value of choosing me to provide those services. Bottom line: I will now be utilizing the X Factor Selling System to close a greater percentage of new client referrals.

As for salespersons in general, Tom La Vecchia's book, The X Factor Selling System, is a MUST HAVE. After having read his book before he appeared on Business Beat Live (I generally wait until after their TV show appearance) I can both heartedly endorse and recommend his book to any person: those desiring to get into sales and those already in the sales field. A small investment in the book will certainly pay huge dividends in return.

FREQUENTLY ASKED QUESTIONS TO THE SALES EXPERT

Q: Is the X Factor process only for outside and inside sales representatives?

A: The answer to that is an emphatic No. This process could be used in various areas of your organization. Whether-be customer service, a marketing group, or even an operational group that is supporting a sales or marketing function. Very often the operational s tor is content with simply putting a square peg in a squa h . Now although this is correct they may be functioning in a secluded environment; it is critical for operations personnel to understand the X Factor of the departments they are serving. So all of the areas of your organization can make use of this process in order to better understand the customers they are servicing and to see the bigger picture.

Q: This is a pretty aggressive sales style. Is this only limited to maybe the Northeast, maybe big cities and maybe possibly the West coast?

A: I believe that is categorically false. My experience is that sales people are forthright because we are often clear about our goals. Although at times we are self-serving, we're pretty clear about what we want because we ask for the business. You control your tone. Asking questions is not inappropriate, however how you ask it could be. So with that being said this is not limited to any part of the country, this is something that can be used globally. Depending on the culture there could be some fine tuning, in terms of tone and such. It's important to ask questions appropriately, but it's okay to be direct. In every culture there is something motivating that person.

Q: How did you increase the plastic surgeon's business four-fold?

A: It was a fairly simple formula. We installed the right people, they followed the X Factor process to a "T" as was taught in their training, and they got on board with the right products. They priced the products correctly, they put packages in place to up-sell and cross-sell, and they used the simple formula of the four P's. So they put it together with the right balance and they achieved a four fold increase in the aesthetic market place, which is a cash business, during one of our worst recessionary periods ever.

Q: How is your process different?

A: Most companies spend millions of dollars on processes that have sales reps focus on overcoming objections; It's like "hey, I don't want to buy X and this is why," and you overcome that objection and you say "great!" and you land a sale and walk away. But they don't really get to the heart of the matter which is the root cause of why people do things- and that's what the X Factor is about. We find out what motivates someone and then we stimulate their motivating factor to make a decision; therefore we create a longer bond with that client and not just a one-off sale. That's the biggest difference.

Q: Do I need to attend a seminar?

A: Yes and no. On one end the book is great. But I would hope that you do attend a seminar. Practice, Practice, Practice. The seminars give you the opportunity to practice the X Factor Selling System in its true form and in a learning environment. The seminars will also provide valuable information to further understand the system in order to implement the method, to customize your goals, and you can meet new and fun people. Also, we are launching our website, thesalesexpertusa.com and other various modules from that platform that can be used. We really feel that the book is great, and it's a foundation, but this is a living and breathing model and it can go as deep as you want or as superficial as you want. But one thing is critical; you really need to practice this model in order to be successful.

Q: I'm not a salesperson, I hate selling, will this work for me?

A: I don't think it's really that people don't like to sell; I think it's that people just don't like to hear "No". I don't like to hear no, people don't like to be shot down. It's just a simple fact of life. But if you follow our model it will facilitate better discussions and frankly fruitful discussions because you will be asking better questions in order to meet certain goals. I don't like to sell; I don't like to persuade people to do something that they don't want to do. My goal is to find out what is going on, to identify any possible deficits or needs that they may have, get them to agree to that deficit or need, and work to meet a goal to correct it. I think it's pretty straightforward and that's what the top sales reps do.

Q: Why do most sales reps fail?

A: Well it's one of two things: lack of desire to succeed or lack of skill. We can't teach you how to want but if the desire is there we can train you to win with successful practices.

EXERCISES

Exercise 1

Pair up into two teams. Prepare a series of notecards with a P category, a setting, and an X Factor on each one. You may use the 'possible X Factors' from the manual or you may choose to make up your own. If this is in an office setting you may choose to do this exercise with your actual products.

Example of a Notecard:

Location: Car dealership

P Category: Price

X Factor: Feels getting the lowest cost means good business.

Pair up a player from team A and team B and have one person from team A look at a notecard. The person without the notecard will ask questions to try and figure out what P Category the other person falls under and guess their X Factor. Switch on and off between the two teams.

Thomas F. La Vecchia

Optional:

If you would like to play for points:

3 points-guessed the other person's P category and X Factor correctly

2 points -guessed the other persons X Factor correctly

1 point- guessed the other persons P category correctly

0 points-guessed neither correctly

Purpose of the exercise: to practice asking questions in a learning environment. The more you practice asking the right questions, the better you will become at finding a customer's X Factor.

Exercise 2

Split up into pairs. Designate a buyer and a seller in each pair. On two notecards write a description of the buyer on one and the seller on the other.

For example:

NOTECARD 1: Buyer: price centric with an X Factor of not having a substantial financial plan in place to spend more to make more later on. Only wants to spend $15 per unit of cookies.

NOTECARD 2: Seller: has a goal to sell cookies at a price of $20 per unit.

Have one team at a time role-play getting to the close of a deal. The seller must gain alignment with the buyer and to get them to meet their goal while also fulfilling their X Factor.

Optional:
Create two teams out of your overall group. This way, each person is playing to gain the most sales for their team. You can pair up one buyer from one team and one seller from the other team for each "sale".

Purpose of the Exercise: to learn how to gain alignment with a buyer. The value of using the X Factor Selling System is due to mutual success through increased partnership between the buyer and the seller. Understanding how to not only find the buyer's X Factor, but to align goals, is the key to this process.

<u>**Exercise 3**</u>

Have everyone come up with an advertisement; this advertisement can be for your company, the product your company sells, or for a made up product/seminar, etc. Have each person create the advertisement using the three critical components. Have each person present their advertisement to the group.

Or, present an advertisement or advertisements from your company. Knowing what your sales team knows about the product (from listening to clients and talking with the consumer face-to-face) ask them what changes they would make to the ad or ads.

Optional:
After each person presents their advertisement, have the rest of the group vote on whether they felt a call to action from the ad or if they would buy the product/attend the seminar.

Purpose of the exercise: the marketing department and the sales team should have an understanding of one another. Having your sales team create an advertisement, or give feedback on your company's current ad, can be a helpful exercise in seeing the bigger picture. Also, obtaining input from your sales team about marketing your current product can be helpful-they speak directly to the customers and know what features catch a buyer's attention.

Exercise 4

Have each person think about what has motivated them, or what they need to motivate them, to succeed. Have them write down what has motivated in the past or currently and what success they've reached because of that. Or, have them right down what they would like in order to motivate them, and how that motivation will help them to be more successful.

Next, have them email you their answers after the exercise and meet with them individually to see how you can work to provide that motivation for them. Gain alignment with each person on their goals. After they receive the motivation, touch back with them after an agreed upon time to measure their results.

Purpose of this exercise: It is crucial to know what motivates your team. Motivating factors may vary for each person, so it is important to meet individually in order to find that out. Gaining alignment on their goals after they receive their motivation will produce a more successful working environment. Also, it is important for each person to recognize and know what their motivating factor is.

Exercise 5

Have each person present to the rest of the group some of their daily or weekly goals that they use to provide successful results. Also have them provide mistakes they have made that have led to fruitless results.

Purpose of the exercise: Sharing successes and failures is a constructive way for a team to learn from one another. Although not everyone's success will look the same-or their process and/or metrics-it provides a learning environment and sounding board.

BIBLIOGRAPHY

Tzu, Sun. *The Art of War*. London: Oxford UP,1971.

Merriam-Webster's Dictionary, "passion."

Greene, Robert and Joost Elffers. *The 48 Laws of Power*.
New York: Penguin, 2000.

ABOUT THE AUTHOR

Thomas F. La Vecchia, MBA, aka "The Sales Expert," is the creator of the X Factor Selling System. He has worked in the pharmaceutical/medical device space in both the individual contributor role and in sales leadership. He has won more than ten national sales awards and has led his colleagues to win another ten awards. He has his Masters of Business Administration from Fairleigh Dickinson University in Hackensack New Jersey and his undergraduate degree from Rutgers University. Thomas's accomplishments during his twenty years of corporate experience include bringing up regional sales teams to top ranking positions, as well as coaching and developing high performance sales professionals. He has presented internationally on various sales topics and is now sharing his "secret sauce" with the rest of the world. Thomas was born and raised in New Jersey and currently lives in the northern New Jersey area with his wife Rosalia and his two children, Felicia and Giuseppe. His goal for unveiling the X Factor Selling System is to inspire greatness.

You can learn more about the X Factor Selling System by vising the following:

www.TheSalesExpertUSA.com

Twitter @TheSalesExpert

The "X Factor Selling Systems" Facebook Page

X Factor Selling Systems WordPress Blog